AF430497

I Can Read Kids Book Club
www.iCanReadKids.com

Read Aloud

Short, simple words and sentences. Repetitive vocabulary and full-color illustrations for children at the very first stages of learning to read.

Read Along

Short sentences, repetitive vocabulary, simple concepts for your child to learn how to read with a little help.

Read With Help

Engaging stories, longer sentences, and less repetitive vocabulary increased wordplay for developing readers who still need some help.

Read Alone

More complex stories, challenging vocabulary, and engaging plots for the solo reader.

Read Advanced

Advanced plots and vocabulary. Short paragraphs and short chapters based on exciting themes.

iCanReadKids.com
Level
4
Reader
(Age 9-12)
iCan Read Kids Book Club

Hey, I'm a time traveler from the future.
I traveled back in time to tell you all about how money works in my time.

Before I explain the future of money, let's take a look at how money worked in the past and how money works in your time.

A long time ago, before money was invented, people had to trade on a thing for another, to get all the things they wanted.

Exchanging a thing for another thing is called Bartering or the Barters System. Here is how it worked; let's say. Larry, the Lumber Jack, has more wood than he can use, and Ellen, the Egg Farmer, has more eggs than she can eat.

Both Larry and Ellen have more than they need, so they decide to trade the extra amounts for other things they want.

After chopping wood, all-day Larry is very hungry, and Ellen needs firewood to cook her eggs. Both Larry and Ellen need something from each other, so they start trading. Ellen will trade eggs to Larry for firewood.

Ellen and Larry will determine an exchange rate of how many pieces of wood is equal to each egg. They may decide that 2 eggs = 1 piece of wood. The exchange rate could change depending on the season and supply and demand. Supply and demand is a way to explain the relationship between quantity and desire. When Larry has a lot of wood, he may offer Ellen more wood for each egg. If something were to happen, such as if a forest fire burned down many trees, then Larry could demand more eggs because there is a lower supply of wood available for all the people who also want wood.

If wolves ate some of Ellen's chickens and she has fewer eggs to trade, she could ask Larry for more wood in exchange for each egg. Another example of supply and demand since Ellen doesn't have enough eggs to trade with all the people who want eggs.

But the barter system had a problem!

The problem with the barter system is that if you can't find someone who wants what you have and also has what you want, then you can't trade.

Let's say Ellen wants apples from Adam the Apple Farmer, but Adam needs firewood. To get apples, Ellen would first have to trade for firewood and then trade for Apples. Trading becomes complicated when more than two people are involved in the trade.

Eventually, money was invented to make trading with anyone at any time easier. Money is something that everyone can use to trade for anything they want; this is called the monetary system.

In the past, people used many things as money. Some of the things that were used as money in the past are shells, salt, and even animals. People kept trying to find something that could be the perfect money.

In 600 BC, sliver and gold coins became the most common form of money used for trade. Gold and silver coins remained the ultimate money for over 2500 years.

Gold and silver were the most durable thing that has been used as money. But it wasn't perfect.

As the world started to get more connected, and people started trading in markets that were far away. Gold and silver coins was just too heavy to carry around in large amounts.

People also needed someplace safe to keep their gold and silver, so banks were created. Banks charge fees for holding other people's gold or money. The Bankers became wealthy by being the middlemen between people trading with each other. The banking system became the main focus of the monetary system in your time. Banks introduced paper money and credit cards.

BANK

People use paper money and credit cards to buy the things they want, like food, clothes, and toys. The system worked pretty well but it still wasn't perfect, and it caused a lot of problems that we figured out how to solve in the future. Banks became too big and expensive to operate. They have to pay for large office buildings, lots of employees, lawyers, so they charged a lot of fees for using their service. Banks also were not able to keep people's money completely safe.

As society became, more modern people started realizing that banks and credit card companies were makings trading slower and more expensive. Banks began to limit how people can use their money and how much of their money they can spend.

WANT ME TO HOLD THAT FOR YOU?
NAHH!! I CAN DO IT BY MYSELF!

THIS IS FOR ME!
AH?
THIS IS YOUR PART!

One of the hidden ways that the modern banking system made things more expensive is called inflation. Inflation means that the money you have is worth a little less each day.

Inflation is why an ice cream cone cost $0.05 in 1950 but costs $5.00 in 2020. It's not that the ice cream cone increased in value; it's that the money has declined in value.

The Bankers made sure that the value of paper money declines to less than the face value by charging interest on every single dollar they print. As they print more and more money to circulate in society, it's value decrease even more. The more of something there is, the less scarce it is, making it less valuable. When something is scarce, it means supply is low, and there is not enough for all the people who want it, so it's worth more because people are willing to offer more to get it.

Remember what happened when wolves ate some of Ellen's chickens, and she had fewer eggs to trade? She demanded more wood in exchange for each egg.

In the same way, when bankers print more money, they cause the value of all money to decline.

I LOVE MONEY!

Eventually, some brilliant people came up with the perfect features that would make money perfect.

Coders started using technology to create the perfect money. Money that would be safe, fast, and cheap.

It would be sent directly from one person to another, anywhere in the world without needing a bank or middlemen. There would be no limits, and it would be completely private.

It would be scarce with a limited supply to create the opposite effect of inflation called deflation. This means the value of the money is designed to increase over time or be stable.

People would be able to send it in large or tiny amounts, it would be easy to carry, everyone would know what it is, and impossible to destroy.

MONEY MUST HAVE THESE FIVE CHARACTERISTICS:

1. MONEY MUST BE DIVISIBLE

2. MONEY MUST BE PORTABLE

3. MONEY MUST BE DURABLE

4. MONEY MUST BE RECONGNIZABLE

5. MONEY MUST BE SCARCE

DONE!

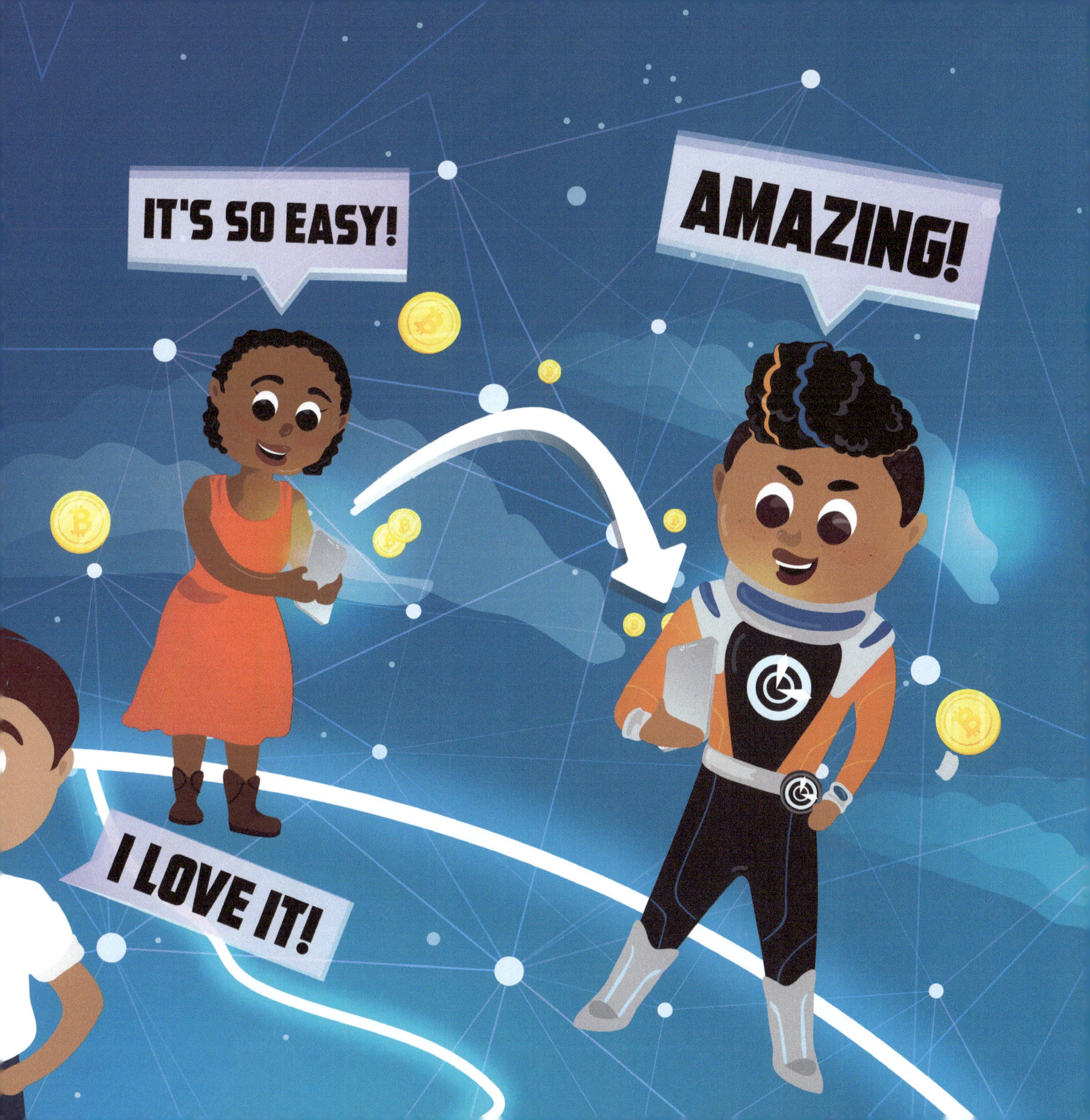

IT'S SO EASY!
AMAZING!
I LOVE IT!

The money we use in the future
is called cryptocurrency.

In the future, where I am from, money is not printed, there are no dollar bills, no metal coins, and no cards – it's 100% digital! Everything is done with phones and computers. This allows for fast and cheap transactions. It can be used by anyone, anywhere in the world. There are no dollars, euros, pesos, or yen - it's a world currency.

The cryptocurrency money was created by coders. It uses cryptography to securely send payments. Cryptography is a technology that protects information through complex math functions and currency is another way to say money. Money in the future uses strong cryptography to protect your account and let you securely send money. It can't be hacked.

So now you know all about the money from the past, present and future.

YEP! IS DONE!
SUPER EASY!

NOW IT'S TIME TO GO BACK
TO THE FUTURE. BYE!

www.iCanReadKids.com
Book club for young readers age 0-12